Genetic Engineering

Critical World Issues

CRITICAL WORLD ISSUES

Genetic Engineering

Martin Thompson

MASON CREST
PHILADELPHIA

Mason Crest
450 Parkway Drive, Suite D
Broomall, PA 19008
www.masoncrest.com

Printed and bound in the United States of America.

CPSIA Compliance Information: Batch #CWI2016.
For further information, contact Mason Crest at 1-866-MCP-Book.

First printing
1 3 5 7 9 8 6 4 2

Library of Congress Cataloging-in-Publication Data

on file at the Library of Congress
ISBN: 978-1-4222-3655-0 (hc)
ISBN: 978-1-4222-8135-2 (ebook)

Critical World Issues series ISBN: 978-1-4222-3645-1

Table of Contents

KEY ICONS TO LOOK FOR:

 Words to Understand: These words with their easy-to-understand definitions will increase the reader's understanding of the text, while building vocabulary skills.

 Sidebars: This boxed material within the main text allows readers to build knowledge, gain insights, explore possibilities, and broaden their perspectives by weaving together additional information to provide realistic and holistic perspectives.

 Research Projects: Readers are pointed toward areas of further inquiry connected to each chapter. Suggestions are provided for projects that encourage deeper research and analysis.

 Text-Dependent Questions: These questions send the reader back to the text for more careful attention to the evidence presented there.

 Series Glossary of Key Terms: This back-of-the book glossary contains terminology used throughout this series. Words found here increase the reader's ability to read and comprehend higher-level books and articles in this field.

Introduction
to Genetics

Naomi works for a company in Europe that conducts scientific research on *genes*, the parts of a cell that control the characteristics of a living thing. She tries to find out what genes do and how to change, or "engineer," them. This is called *genetic engineering* or genetic modification. Here is Naomi's story:

"When I was at school ten years ago, I loved science. Everyone said that science would be very important in the future—especially computers and genetics. For my work in genetics, I deal mainly with chemicals in flasks and test tubes. I also have to use machines which separate genes, identify them, and copy them. I'm a small part of a big team. I'm only involved in some of the work because genetics is a very complicated process.

Scientists in a genetic engineering laboratory monitor the development of genetically modified seedlings from an agricultural crop. Genetic engineering is not only confined to the laboratory; it can affect the food that is grown all around the world.

"To put it simply, genes are bits of chemicals inside a living thing, and they are like instructions. They tell a living thing how to grow, survive, and carry out its life processes. In our research, we find genes in one type of living thing which might be useful if we put them into another.

"At the moment, I am studying genes in a weed that grows in wheat fields. Sometimes insects eat the wheat, but they don't eat the weed. We're trying to find out if this is due to a certain gene in the weed. We might be able to put that gene into wheat, so that the insect can no longer damage the crop. That would save farmers money and might even make bread cheaper.

"Our research could last for years, or it might just reach a dead end. The weed has thousands of genes, and it takes ages

 Words to Understand in This Chapter

centrifuge—a machine that uses spinning force, away from the center, to separate substances or parts of substances of different densities.

DNA—deoxyribonucleic acid: a molecule that carries genetic information in the cells of plants and animals.

gel electrophoresis—a process in which an electromotive force moves molecules (as proteins and nucleic acids) through a gel and separates them into bands according to size.

genes—a part of a cell that controls or influences the appearance, growth, etc., of a living thing.

genetic engineering—the science of making changes to the genes of a plant or animal to produce a desired result.

GMO—genetically modified organism: a plant or animal whose genetic material has been altered by genetic engineering.

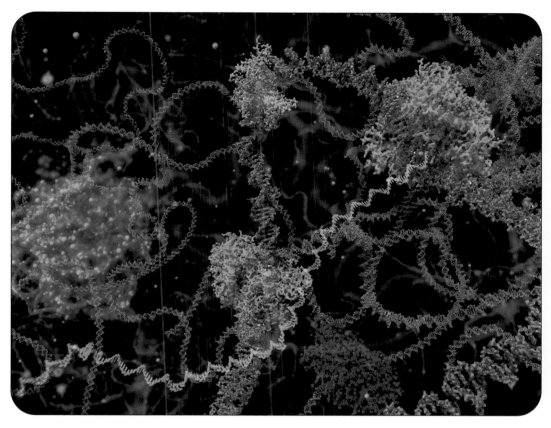

Under a powerful microscope, pieces of DNA look like fuzzy threads or lengths of string.

to study them all. When we move a gene into a different type of living thing, it might not work properly in its new 'home.' And we have to be very careful about safety. Genes are just tiny scraps of chemicals, but some people believe that if they get into the wrong place, they might create a new germ or even a dangerous mutant.

"A few years ago, genetic engineering promised so much. We were going to feed the hungry, heal the sick, and save the world. Progress is happening, but it's very slow. And almost anything to do with genetics seems to cause all kinds of arguments and protests."

DNA and Genes

Imagine that you have to build a complex machine from thousands of parts. To fit them together, you need a set of instructions. A living organism is far more complicated than any machine. It has billions of parts that work together. It also needs a set of instructions, so it can grow, develop, and survive.

The instructions for a machine are usually written on paper. Those for a living thing are in the form of a molecule called deoxyribonucleic acid (*DNA*), a sequence of codes that exists in every cell. In 1953, James Watson and Francis Crick discovered that DNA looks like a long ladder twisted into the shape of a corkscrew called a double-helix. The double-helix shape plays an important role in the way a gene is copied so that its product can be made.

If DNA is the "instruction book," genes are like individual pages of the book that explain how to make specific parts of the machine: in the DNA sequence of codes, genes make up sections of that code sequence. A machine's instructions are big enough for us to see, but genes are so tiny they can only be seen by using special microscopes. All the genes for a living thing, from a daisy or worm to a tree or a whale, are in pieces of DNA that could fit onto the period at the end of this sentence.

How Genes Work

All living things are made of cells, which are like building blocks. Cells are so small that about 10,000 would fit inside this

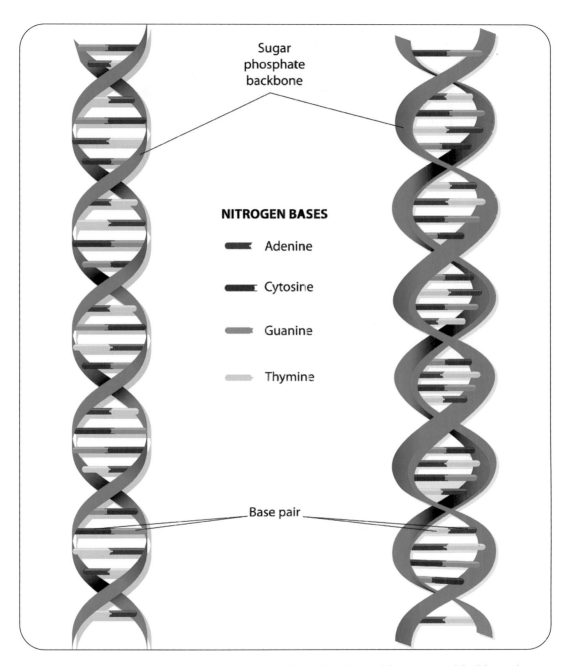

Sugar
phosphate
backbone

NITROGEN BASES

Adenine

Cytosine

Guanine

Thymine

Base pair

DNA has two long strands which make a double-helix shape, like a twisted ladder. The bases that make up the "letters" for the code of genetic information are like the rungs of the ladder.

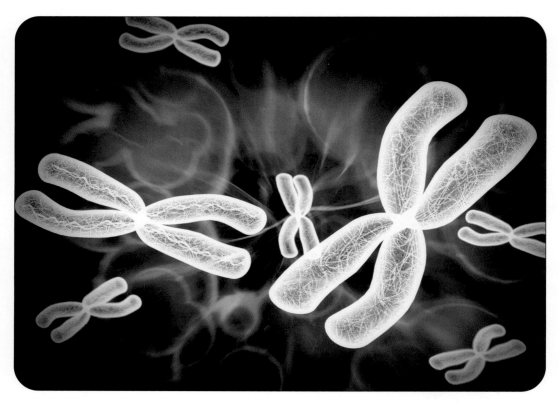

Each double strand of DNA is coiled into loops, and these are, in turn, coiled into larger super-loops. The super-loops are tightly packed to form an X-shaped body called a chromosome. Each microscopic cell in the human body contains 46 of these chromosomes.

"o." There are 37.2 trillion cells in a human body, but a gene section of DNA is even smaller than a cell: to a gene, a cell is like a gigantic "living factory."

Each DNA strand is made up of smaller pieces, or subunits called bases, which are joined together in a long row like beads on a necklace. In the same way that a word carries information by the order of its letters, a DNA carries information by the order of its bases which form a code. We use 26 different letters to make words, but DNA has only 4 different bases: adenine

(A), guanine (G), cytosine (C), and thymine (T). Genes make up sections of the DNA double helix, and each gene has hundreds or thousands of bases in sequence, so it can carry a huge amount of information. The whole set of human genes has 3.1 billion pairs of bases.

For a gene to work, the order of its bases is copied into another substance very similar to DNA, called ribonucleic acid (RNA). The RNA then goes to another place inside the cell, where it carries out its job, almost like a person in a factory. It gathers together various substances or raw materials and fixes them together in the right order, following the instructions in

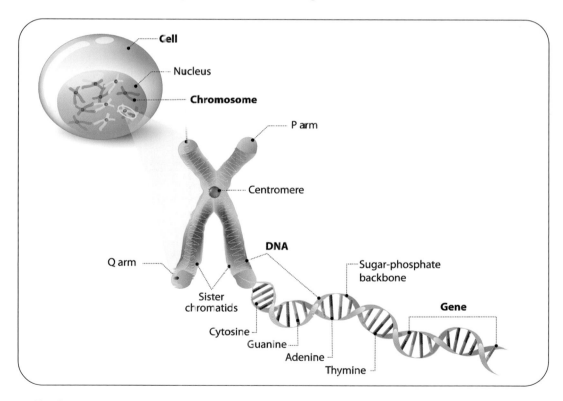

Cell, Chromosome, DNA and gene. A gene is a length of DNA that codes for a specific protein, and is contained in the chromosomes that are part of each cell.

the original gene.

The result of this process is a product—a substance, or protein, in the body. An example is the substance that gives the eyes their color. In one person, the product is blue, so the eyes are blue. We say that the person has the gene for blue eyes. In

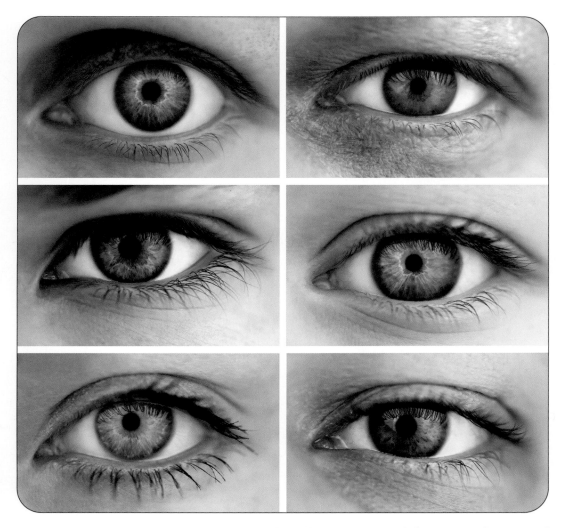

Eye color is determined by a certain gene. The different versions of the gene produce eyes of different colors.

another person the gene for eye color has a slightly different order of bases. This gives a brown product for brown eyes.

A whole human body has about 19,000 different types of genes. Every tiny cell contains all of these genes. But in any single cell, only some of the genes are "switched on." The rest are "switched off." In the cells at the front of the eye, the genes for eye color are "on" and make their product while other genes are "off" and make nothing. The fact that all the cells contain all the types of genes is very important in genetic engineering.

Genetic Engineering

Every plant or animal, such as an apple tree or a sheep, has a set of thousands of genes within its DNA, which resembles tiny threads of pale jelly. This DNA can be taken out by chemical means. In genetic engineering, the DNA is split into shorter pieces, each of which is studied to see which particular genes it contains. Then a gene can be altered, moved, removed, or put into the DNA of another living thing.

Genes can be separated, studied, and joined back together by manipulating DNA, the molecule that contains the genes.

To obtain genes, you need just a tiny piece of a living thing such as a strand of hair, a flake of skin, or a flower petal. Even such a tiny piece contains millions of cells, and every cell contains the full set of the living thing's genes.

The first step to identifying genes is to heat the cells with chemicals to make them release their contents. These are then spun around very fast in a *centrifuge* machine (like a spin dryer), which separates them into different layers. The DNA

A centrifuge machine is charged with samples—a key step in the process of extracting DNA.

layer is thin and pale and looks like damp cotton. Its threads can be wound onto a glass rod.

The long lengths of DNA are split into shorter ones by warming them with various proteins called restriction enzymes (REs). These short fragments of DNA are identified by adding them to yet more proteins, putting them in a clear gel, and passing electricity through the gel. This makes various fragments move different distances along the gel. Called *gel electrophoresis*, this process creates a row of lines that look like a supermarket barcode. This identifies the DNA piece and so identifies the gene.

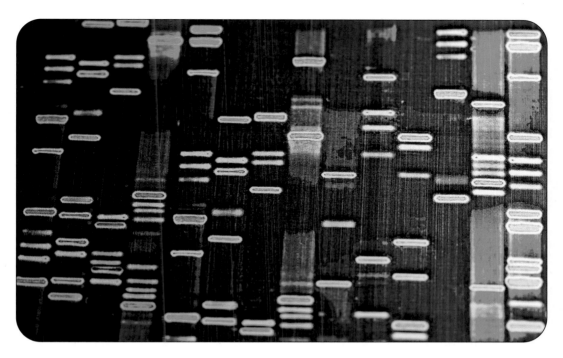

Pieces of DNA reveal their codes as patterns of dark bars, in the laboratory test called gel electrophoresis.

Adding Genes to Living Things

The fragments of DNA are genes or parts of genes. Once identified for their properties, the genes can be added to the DNA of another living thing by using microscopic lifeforms called phages to "carry" them. The phages, which are a type of virus, are put in a flask with copies of the new gene. Some of them take the new gene into themselves. The phages are then added to other cells such as those of an animal.

Phages are so small that they can get into a cell and add the new gene to it. The altered cell is then encouraged to divide and make more cells like itself. As it divides and makes more cells, it can even be made to develop into a whole living thing. This new living thing is called a transgenic lifeform or genetically modified organism (*GMO*).

Benefits and Risks of Genetic Engineering

Suppose that scientists study a plant that grows many large seeds. They take out and identify the genes that make the seeds big and numerous. Then they add these genes into another type of plant, where they do not occur naturally. The genes work in their new "home," and the second plant grows more and bigger seeds. If this plant is a farm crop, this process is, of course, very helpful to the farmer. But genetics is hugely complex. Things can go wrong and often do. The rewards may be great, but there could be dangers involved that we cannot even imagine until they happen.

Text-Dependent Questions

1. Explain the difference between DNA and genes.
2. Describe the steps involved in genetic engineering.

 # Research Project

When blue light shines on Alba the rabbit, she glows green. The reason for this is that Alba was given a gene from a jellyfish. This gene makes the jellyfish glow naturally in the dark ocean. Alba was created as "living art" by Eduardo Kac. She seems healthy and happy, but is this type of genetic engineering acceptable?

Using the Internet or your school library, research the topic of bioart, and answer the following question: "Is it right to use genetic engineering to create art out of animals?"

Some claim that it is acceptable because art is an expression of truth and life, and making art out of animals can be beautiful while making a social statement. If the creatures are not harmed, this is no different from established entities like zoos and even modeling, which use living things for expression or awareness.

Others contend that it is wrong to make unnatural changes to animals that have to undergo medical procedures for something that is not beneficial to them. People do not treat other people in such ways, and animals should not be used to merely entertain humans.

Write a two-page report, using data you have found in your research to support your conclusion, and present it to your class.

2

Genetic Disorders

Every human body starts as a tiny egg cell inside its mother's womb. This egg cell contains all the genes it needs to grow and develop into a newborn baby and then a full-grown human. But in a few cases, there is an alteration in the genes that impacts the genes' instructions for making proteins that do the work in cell development. The result may be a *genetic disorder* which affects health and normal life. About 1 to 2 babies in every 100 are born with a genetic disorder.

The genes for the human body are instructions, not only for the finished body, but for the developing and growing process too. If there is a tiny alteration, such as a missing gene or one which is slightly abnormal, the body may not be able to develop or work normally.

◄━━━━━━━━━━━━━━━━━━━━━━━━━━━━━━━

Each child receives a unique set of genes from its two parents (apart from identical twins, which have the same genes).

There are thousands of different genetic disorders. Some have little effect on health, although they may be noticeable. Examples are a red mark on the skin, called a birthmark, or an extra finger or toe. Other genetic disorders can cause serious health problems. If the heart does not develop in the normal way, for example, it may not pump blood through the body effectively.

Genetic Mutations

At the start of development, the single egg cell splits into two cells. Then each of these cells also divides into two, and so on. The total number of cells becomes 4, 8, 16, 32, and gradually increases to hundreds, thousands, and millions to build the growing body.

 Words to Understand in This Chapter

dominant gene—a gene that produces its characteristic traits in the organism whether or not it is paired with an identical gene.

gene therapy—a way of treating some disorders and diseases that usually involves replacing mutated copies of genes with healthy genes that have been engineered.

genetic disorder—a medical condition in which a genetic mutation changes the gene's instructions for making a protein, so the protein does not work properly or is missing entirely.

mutation—a relatively permanent change in genetic material.

recessive gene—a gene that produces its characteristic traits only when it is paired with an identical gene.

stem cell—a simple cell in the body that is able to develop into any one of various kinds of cells (such as blood cells, skin cells, etc.).

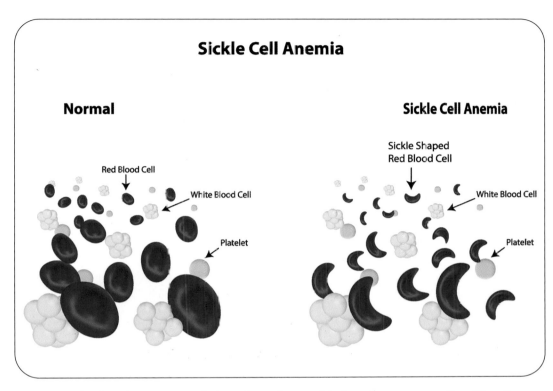

Sickle Cell Anemia

Normal

Red Blood Cell

White Blood Cell

Platelet

Sickle Cell Anemia

Sickle Shaped
Red Blood Cell

White Blood Cell

Platelet

Some genetic disorders are not obvious from the outside, but they can greatly affect the way the body works. We breathe in and out to get oxygen from the air, and the oxygen is carried around the body by our blood. In a genetic disorder called sickle-cell anemia, the blood cannot carry this oxygen properly, resulting in severe illness or death.

Every time a cell divides, its full set of genes is copied. This happens because the lengths of DNA which form the genes make exact copies of themselves. So the two cells from every division each have a full set of genes.

Very rarely, this copying process goes wrong. A gene can get altered, missed out, or put into the wrong place in the whole set. This change is called a *mutation*. Often, the reasons for this are unknown, but in some cases, there is a known cause that interferes with gene copying, including germs, harmful drugs and chemicals, and dangerous rays such as radioactive waves.

Inherited Genetic Disorders

A human body can develop a genetic disorder as it grows in the mother's womb, after birth, or even later in life. But in some cases, the disorder is there at the beginning in the tiny, fertilized egg cell. It has been passed on from one or both parents. This is known as an inherited genetic disorder, and it can happen in various ways.

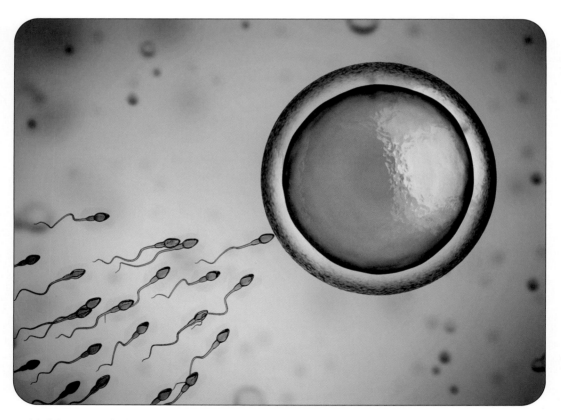

A highly magnified view of the egg and sperm cells from which a new human body will grow.

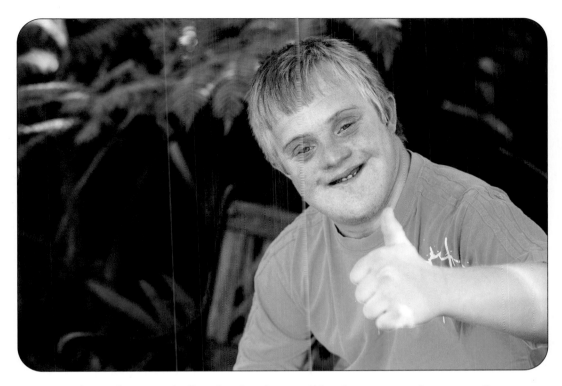

Down syndrome is a genetic disorder that is caused by the presence of an extra chromo-some. This random mutation is among the more common genetic disorders, affecting about 1 in 1,000 children.

The fertilized egg cell contains two sets of human genes. One set comes from the mother, who produced the egg cell. The other set comes from the father, who produced the sperm cell. During fertilization, the sperm cell joins with the egg cell, and because the fertilized egg cell has two full sets of genes, every cell in the resulting body also has both sets. In other words, the genes occur in pairs.

Sometimes one gene in a pair is altered, but the other one is normal. In certain cases, the normal gene is allowed to work in the usual way because the mutated gene "gives in." A gene that gives in is called a *recessive gene*. In other cases, the affected gene of a pair does not "give in" and in fact "takes over." It does not allow the normal gene to work properly, so a problem results. This type of altered gene that takes over is known as a *dominant gene*. It can cause conditions such as tuberous sclerosis, which affects the skin and brain.

On very rare occasions, both parents may pass a mutated recessive gene to their baby. So the baby receives a pair of genes, one from each parent, and both are altered. In this case, there is no normal version available to make the recessive gene "give in." This can create conditions such as sickle-cell anemia.

There are more than 1,500 different medical disorders caused by a mutation in a single gene inherited from a parent. There are thousands more that are caused not by one mutated gene but by two or more. These are described as "multiple-gene disorders."

In the Family

It is known that genes play a part in many conditions and illnesses, but it is not always clear how many genes are involved or exactly how they cause the problem. It is simply too complicated to work out at this point. Examples are the breathing problems of asthma, skin disorders of eczema, various allergies, and certain types of heart disease. We say that the condition "runs in the family," while doctors might say there is "an inherited tendency" or "a genetic component."

Genetic disorders vary greatly in the ways that they are passed from parent to child and in their effects on health and well-being. But there are many ways to predict them, detect

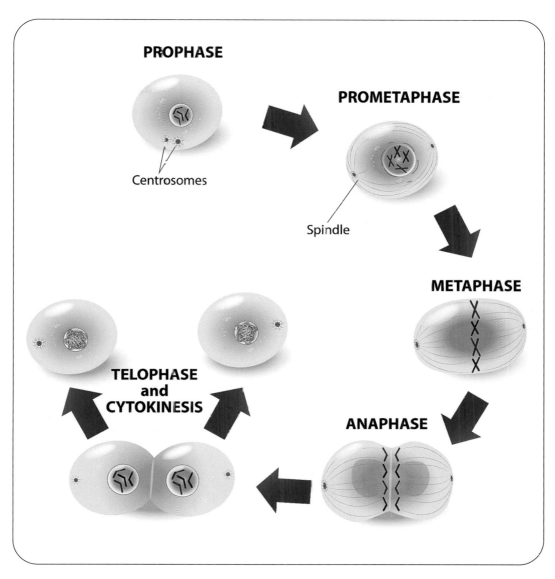

PROPHASE

Centrosomes

PROMETAPHASE

Spindle

METAPHASE

TELOPHASE and CYTOKINESIS

ANAPHASE

Mitosis, or cell division, is the process by which our bodies replace cells. There are six stages in mitosis. Just before a cell divides, the chromosomes appear from the nucleus and double in number (prophase). Each pair then lines up along the middle of the cell (prometaphase). Next the members of each pair are pulled towards opposite end of the cell (metaphase). The sister chromatids move to opposite poles of the cell (anaphase), and a new nucleus is formed in each of the new cells (telophase). Finally the cell divides (cytokinesis). Both the new cells will have exactly the same number of chromosomes as there were in the original cell, and genetic material remains constant.

them if they occur, and treat them.

Sometimes genetic disorders can be predicted by experts called genetic counselors. If an inherited condition has

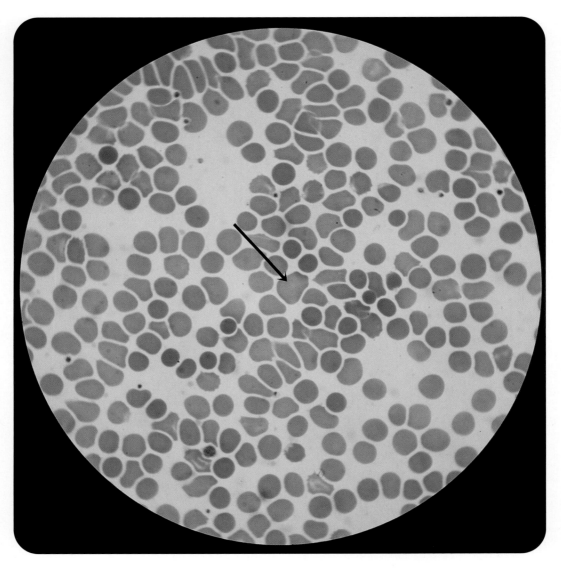

Polychromasia is a disorder where there is an abnormally high number of red blood cells found in the bloodstream as a result of being prematurely released from the bone marrow during blood formation.

occurred in the parents' families, the genetic counselor may be able to figure out the chances that their baby will have it as well. This may be stated in accurate, straightforward terms such as a "three-in-four" risk. If only one parent has the disorder, or it has occurred only in relatives such as brothers or aunts, as opposed to parents, the risk may be less.

Sometimes a counselor advises parents to have tests on their blood or other body parts. As we have seen, genes occur in pairs, and it is possible that one gene of the pair is mutated while the other is normal. Without undergoing tests, the parent might not be aware that he or she "carries" a mutation that might be passed on to their baby.

Treatment of Genetic Disorders

Some genetic disorders can be detected and even treated when the baby is still in the womb. Others can be treated soon after birth by a surgical operation or medicinal drugs. The long-term outlook for the baby could be a normal life. But certain conditions have less optimistic long-term results. These can affect not only the health of the baby as it grows up but also schooling and many aspects of family life.

If a couple knows they have inherited genetic disorders that can be passed on if they try for a baby, they need to discuss the risks and treatment possibilities. Their desire to have a baby may be such that they decide to go forward with the willingness to care for their child, whatever the genetic disorders. They may also consider not having children, adopting a baby, or using sperm or eggs donated from somebody without the mutation.

The genetic counselor is a medically trained doctor who specializes in how conditions are inherited.

Difficult Decisions

Some serious genetic disorders can be detected while the baby is still very tiny in the womb. An example is spina bifida, where the nerves of the spinal cord and brain do not form properly. If this is detected, some parents may consider termination of pregnancy, also known as abortion. But other parents might still have their baby and provide the additional care necessary for their child; even if they do not have a "normal" life, they can still love and grow together as a family, as many have already done.

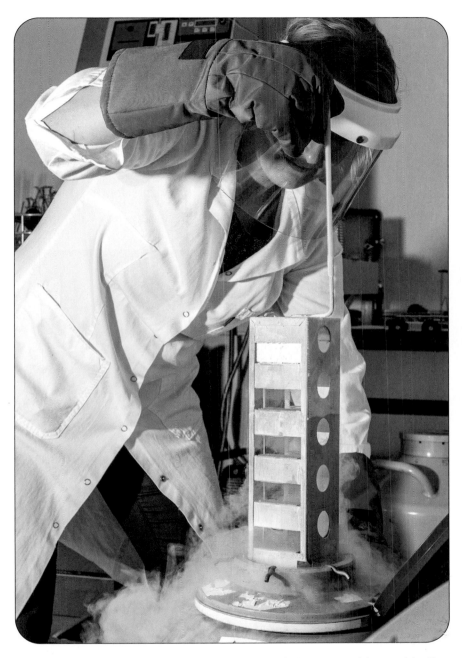

Cells and tissues from people with genetic conditions are cold-stored in liquid nitrogen, so they can be studied. This helps to predict the risk that they will pass the condition to their own children.

Views on this issue vary widely. Some countries offer abortion as part of the medical system, while others legally forbid ending the life of a baby in the womb. Some consider abortion a way of saving a child and their family from suffering. But others, especially in religious faiths, believe every person has their own unique struggles, some severe, but all have a right to life—a mother has the choice to do what she wants with her body in most circumstances but not when it comes to a life and death decision of another human being, even if that human is the baby in her body.

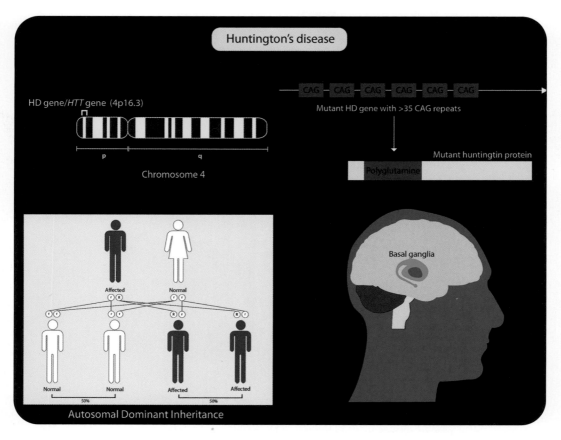

Huntington's disease is a genetic disorder that generally appears in adults. It affects muscle coordination and leads to mental decline and physical disability.

Gene Therapy for Cystic Fibrosis

Cystic fibrosis affects about 1 child in every 2,000. The gene that causes it has been identified as the one that contains the instructions to make the natural slimy mucus that protects the insides of the lungs. But the mutated gene makes the mucus much thicker than normal, clogging the lungs and causing coughing, infections, and many other health problems.

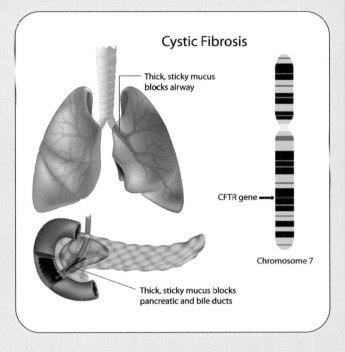

Cystic Fibrosis

Thick, sticky mucus blocks airway

CFTR gene ➝

Chromosome 7

Thick, sticky mucus blocks pancreatic and bile ducts

Gene therapy aims to add the normal mucus-making genes to cells in the lungs with "carriers" such as genetically engineered viruses. However, successful treatment is proving to be difficult: Some lung cells take up the new genes and use them for a time, but eventually these healthy cells wear out and die. They are replaced by cells with the mutated gene, and the problem comes back.

Gene Therapy

A person's genes are inside every microscopic cell of their body. If there is a genetic mutation in the initial egg cell, then every cell will have the same alteration in its genes. Scientists are working on correcting these mutations with a new form of treatment called *gene therapy*.

In almost every body part, millions of tiny new cells are made every day to replace those that wear out and die. With a genetic disorder, all of these cells have the same mutation. In gene therapy, the aim is to correct the mutation by replacing the affected genes with normal ones or to put in new cells that do not contain the altered genes.

Stem Cells

One way around this difficulty is to carry out treatment before birth, when many cells of the body have not yet become specialized to do particular jobs. These unspecialized cells are called *stem cells*. They are more likely to take up engineered genes in a permanent way and allow them to work. Then the genes can pass to all the cells that develop from the stem cells. In the case of cystic fibrosis, normal mucus-making genes might continue to pass to lung cells for years or even a lifetime.

However, this type of treatment means testing a very tiny baby in the womb to see if it has the condition, which brings its own risks and problems. Work on cystic fibrosis and many other genetic disorders has been slow, and some results have been disappointing.

Text-Dependent Questions

1. Explain how a genetic mutation takes place and its effect in the development of a human being.
2. Why might stem cells have a greater success rate in gene therapy than specialized cells?

 # Research Project

If gene therapy becomes possible, it could involve testing tiny babies before birth or even screening single egg cells for genetic problems.

Using the Internet or your school library, research the topic of gene therapy, and answer the following question: "Should gene therapy be allowed?"

Some believe gene therapy should not be legal because it is not natural and may even go wrong. There is beauty in how children develop with unique characteristics, for better or worse. Some disorders can make a person grow in special ways and become even stronger, and society must learn to accept people as they are. There may be no limit to how parents want to "design" their children if gene therapy is allowed.

Others argue that gene therapy should be allowed because it may lead to healthier people who can avoid debilitating medical conditions. People could live longer with a higher quality of life, which benefits the person, their family, and their community. There would be less cost to society in bills to treat medical problems.

Write a two-page report, using data you have found in your research to support your conclusion, and present it to your class.

3

Biotechnology

Biotechnology is both a science and an industry.
Biotechnology combines biology, the science of living
things, with technology, the science of industry and
machines.

In its simple form, biotechnology goes back hundreds of
years. For example, bread is made using tiny living organisms
called yeasts. As bread dough is baked in an oven, the yeasts in
it make a gas called carbon dioxide. This produces tiny bubbles
that make the bread "rise" and develop its distinctive spongy
texture.

Another example of traditional biotechnology is the fer-
menting of beer and wine. Yeasts are again used, and they work
as tiny "living factories." The yeast cells naturally produce
alcohol as a waste substance, which is the most important

*Biotechnology is a broad discipline in which biological processes, organisms, cells
or cellular components are exploited to develop new technologies. New tools and
products developed by biotechnologists are useful in research, agriculture, industry
and the clinic.*

ingredient of beer and wine. The yeast cells make thousands or millions of identical products, just like a factory, but the products are made by living processes, not mechanical ones.

Over hundreds of years, when making bread, beer, and wine, people have chosen which kinds of yeast to use. If a new type of yeast appeared naturally, and it gave tastier bread or better- flavored wine, people saved this yeast and used it again. Sometimes yeasts were mixed together to try to combine the best features of each by combining their genes. This method of choosing or selecting from what is available in nature is called *selective breeding*, or artificial selection. But this process takes a long time and depends greatly on chance.

Quicker Copies

Every time a microscopic cell splits or divides, the DNA of its genes is copied so that each of the two resulting cells receives a

 Words to Understand in This Chapter

biotechnology—the use of living cells, bacteria, etc., to make useful products (such as crops that insects are less likely to destroy or new kinds of medicine).

hormone—a natural substance that is produced in the body and that influences the way the body grows or develops.

immunize—to give someone a vaccine to prevent infection by a disease.

selective breeding—the intentional mating of two animals or plants in an attempt to produce offspring with desirable characteristics or for the elimination of a trait.

splice—to join two things together by connecting their ends.

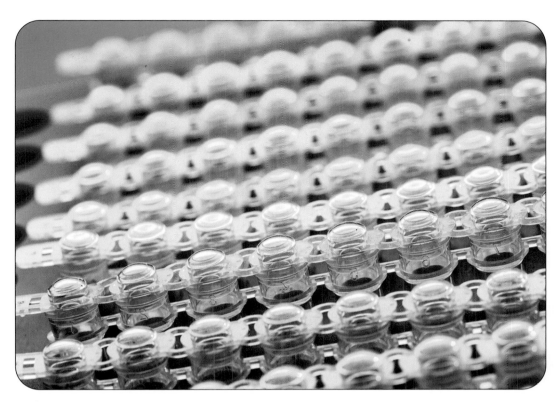

Strands of DNA can be reproduced in a PCR machine. Through a biochemical chain reaction, billions of copies of the DNA can be produced in hours.

full set of genes. This process can be used to produce extra copies of DNA for genetic engineering. But this "cell-growth" method is slow, and sometimes the cells die or have altered DNA. In the late 1980s, a new method was developed called polymerase chain reaction (PCR). This chemical technique is much faster and more reliable than cell growth. It can make a million copies of a gene, as lengths of DNA, in a couple of hours. PCR is now a vital part of genetic research.

Genetically-engineered biotechnology (GE biotech) does not simply use natural types of yeast, bacteria, and other

Genetically engineered microbes grow in a cloudy nutrient fluid, or "soup," in this vessel called a bioreactor. The useful substance they produce is filtered and made pure.

microbes as "living factories." Instead, scientists modify or engineer the genes of these microbes, usually by adding a specific gene from another living thing. This can be done quickly and accurately.

The basics of GE biotech are similar to those of many other genetic methods. A living thing that has a useful product is studied to identify the gene for making that product. This gene is then separated or isolated as one or more pieces of DNA. These DNA strands are then added, or *spliced*, into another life-form, which acts as a living factory and produces the useful product. The microbes produce not only their own useful substances but also substances that are beneficial to human beings.

Growth Hormone

The body's growth is controlled by a natural chemical substance called growth *hormone*. Some people do not have enough growth hormone and grow very slowly, but now they can be given extra growth hormone by injection. Previously, the hormone was obtained from dead bodies at an extremely costly price. Genetically engineered bacteria now make growth hormone in larger amounts for less cost. This means many more affected people can receive treatment and grow normally.

One of the main organisms used in GE biotech is a type of bacterium called E. coli (Escherischia coli). This is a single-celled, rod-shaped lifeform about one-hundredth of a millimeter long. E. coli can be grown quickly and easily in a warm "soup" of nutrients in a large flask or vat. Billions of genetically engineered E. coli in the vat divide every 20 to 30 minutes to keep up their numbers as old ones die. When a new gene is added to them, the E. coli make the product the gene tells them to produce. The product is then filtered, or tapped, from the vat and purified for use.

Key GE Biotech Products

One of GE biotech's early successes was the production of insulin. This is an important hormone because it controls the way the body uses its main energy source, sugar. People who

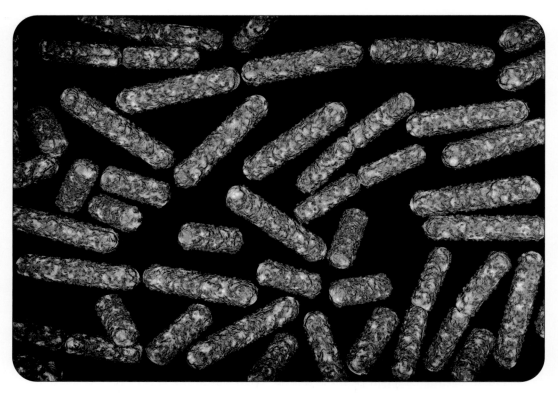

These E. coli bacteria have been genetically altered to make the human hormone insulin. They are shown about 20,000 times larger than life.

lack insulin suffer from a condition called diabetes. They can become very ill or even die.

The normal treatment is to replace the missing insulin with regular injections. Insulin for these injections used to be obtained from farm animals. However, those forms of insulin are slightly different from the human type of insulin. In the 1980s, the gene for making human insulin was identified and put into E. coli bacteria. These bacteria were able to use the gene as their "instructions" and make human insulin for injection.

GE biotech has also been used to produce clotting factor, which can be given to people with the genetic condition called hemophilia, so that their blood clots normally. By using this clotting factor, hemophiliacs avoid the need for blood transfusions, which carry the risk of infections from contaminated blood, such as AIDS and hepatitis.

GE Biotech Medicinal Drugs

In the past few years, there has been a huge amount of research into how new products can be made by genetically engineered organisms. Not only bacteria and similar microbes, but whole plants and animals could be used as living factories.

Some of the most important GE biotech products are medicinal drugs. Microbes have been genetically engineered to make

 Patenting Life

The origin of the business of biotechnology was explained by *Scientific American* magazine: "The biotech industry was spawned when the US Supreme Court ruled in 1980 that it was legal to patent genetically created life." This opened up enormous possibilities for using genetic engineering in commercial business. The first patent in this field was awarded to ExxonMobil Oil Corporation to patent an oil-eating microorganism, which would later be used in the 1989 cleanup of the Exxon oil spill at Prince William Sound, Alaska. Later, patents would be given for such endeavors as gene cloning and genetically-engineered medicines.

antibiotic drugs that kill germs and stop infectious diseases. They can also produce the drug interferon, which treats some diseases caused by viruses and fights certain types of cancer. Some of the vaccines given to babies and children for lifelong protection against diseases are also GE biotech products.

Plants and Animals in GE Biotech

Another area of research is concerned with putting the genes for a medicinal drug, vaccine, or other useful product into a plant grown as food. In this way, people could receive their treatment by eating the food. However, if the genetically-engineered food looks the same as the natural food, people who do not need the treatment might eat it, too, by mistake.

 ## The Biotech Banana

One of the main plant foods for genetic research is the banana. It might be possible to engineer bananas to contain vaccines that *immunize*, or protect, us against diseases. There would be no need for injections—simply eat a genetically-engineered banana! The banana has been chosen because it is widely available, and it comes "packaged" in its skin, which makes it clean and hygienic when eaten. Also, most children and adults like bananas, and they are cheap. A less popular choice would be the genetically-engineered cabbage!

In some European countries, such as Germany, genetically modified organisms (GMO) must be clearly labeled so that consumers know what they are purchasing.

Research has also shown that farm animals such as sheep and goats can be given the genes to make medicinal drugs or similar products. The useful product for humans is obtained from their milk. An example is the drug antithrombin, which stops blood from clotting too much.

Shellfish called mussels stick firmly to rocks, and one hope in biotechnology is that genetically-engineered versions might be gathered and processed to create new kinds of superglue.

Plants such as oilseed rape and sunflowers are grown for their oil. Genetically-engineered forms of these plants might produce oil that can be used in specially-adapted vehicle engines. This could help to reduce air pollution and save motor oil and gas resources.

Genetically-engineered bacteria might also be capable of helping to break down sewage and similar wastes faster than naturally-occurring bacteria. This might lessen the problems of waste disposal and sewage pollution.

Text-Dependent Questions

1. Describe the basic steps involved in using GE biotech.
2. Name two key GE biotech products, two GE biotech medicinal drugs, and two GE biotech benefits from plants and animals.

 # Research Project

GE biotech is a field with many health and practical benefits, but in the wrong hands, it can be used to cause great harm. In recent years, terrorists and national governments in countries like Syria have used biological agents such as anthrax to inflict disease or death. Using the Internet or your school library, research the topic of biotechnology, and answer the following question: "Do the benefits of biotechnology outweigh the risks?"

Some think that the benefits outweigh the risks because there is ever-increasing advancement in medical GE biotech as well as improvements to other areas such as fuel and sewage systems. Though biological weapons have been used in the past, more lives have been saved than killed by far.

Others say that the risks of biotechnology are too great. Of course there have been benefits in fields such as health, but if terrorists employ GE biotech, they could hurt masses of people and bring fear into everyday life. Also, if GE biotech is not properly monitored, things like medicine can have harmful side effects down the road.

Write a two-page report, using data you have found in your research to support your conclusion, and present it to your class.

Traditional farming involves selective breeding, which has produced domesticated versions of animals such as cows.

Selective breeding uses the natural mating process of two individuals of the same species, so genes can only be altered within the same species. For example, cows cannot breed with sheep. This of course means that a sheep's genes for growing a thick, wooly coat could not be transferred to a cow. But in genetic engineering, in theory, genes can be moved from one species of living thing to almost any other, so a cow could in fact receive a gene from a sheep. It could also receive genes from a whale, an insect, or even a holly bush or a mushroom.

Genetic engineering has created "super salmon" that have a gene for faster growth. In fact, they grow up to six times faster than normal salmon. In the future, they could be farmed in large pools or in giant cages suspended in the sea, as normal salmon are today.

But the important and difficult question is whether the gene would work in its new "home."

Golden Rice

Rice is the main food for more than half of the world's people. A genetically modified (GM) variety called "golden rice" is designed to provide the body with more vitamin A. The World Health Organization estimates that 250 million preschool-aged children have vitamin A deficiency, which is the leading cause of preventable blindness in children. Golden rice could provide millions with the vitamin A they need. Tests in real conditions on the rice, called *field trials*, began in Louisiana in 2004. In 2005, a newly-engineered version was found to contain even more nutrients than the previous version.

Studies continue to be conducted for effectiveness and safety, but there has been opposition along the way: Some say researchers gave test subjects unnatural, higher-fat diets, so the vitamin A levels would come out higher. Others claimed the

A child stands in a field of golden rice in Thailand. As the world's population continues to grow, some experts hope that high-yield GM foods may help alleviate hunger while also reducing the strain on natural resources due to overfishing and other environmental issues.

tests were unethically done on children whose parents did not know the rice was a GM crop or that it was under trial. Many believe that the poor are used as a reason for GM crop development when in fact large corporations are seeking huge profits from GM products like golden rice.

Benefits of GM Crops

Genetic engineering can create crops that are resistant to weed killer sprays, so the sprays can be used to kill weeds without harming the crop. It can allow crops to produce a substance that will deter insects from eating them or make crops resistant to diseases caused by plant viruses. Genetic engineering can also improve the quality and quantity of crops, giving them the advantages of faster growth, bigger yields, and better flavor.

Genetic engineering might allow plants to grow in a wider range of growing conditions. If genetically-engineered wheat could grow in drier soil or survive a short drought, it might grow in places where *organic* wheat, grown without artificial chemicals or GMOs, cannot survive. Food can then be produced in former areas of famine.

Certain genes can control ripening, so all of a crop can be ready to harvest at the same time. Other genes can make soft fruits less prone to damage, marks, and bruises as they are picked, packed, transported, and put on display.

The appearance of a food plant can also be changed, so that apples look shiny and smooth rather than dull and wrinkled. It might even be possible to change the colors of plants and animals by genetic engineering and create "novelty" foods such as blue tomatoes or red peas!

Spread of GM Crops

In 2014, there were 181.5 million hectares of GM crops world-wide, compared to 90 million hectares in 2005 and 1.7 million acres in 1996. Eighteen million farmers are growing GM crops today. The four main GM crops are soybean, cotton, maize, and rapeseed (canola). In 2014, GM crops made up 82 percent of the 111 million hectares of the soybean planted globally; 68 percent of the 37 million hectares of cotton; 30 percent of the 184 million hectares of maize; and 25 percent of the 36 million hectares of canola.

However, by no means are all GM crops being grown by ordinary farmers in ordinary fields as food for people. Some are

Savor the Flavor

One of the first genetically-engineered foods to go on sale to the public was the Flavr-Savr tomato. It was introduced into 730 stores in the United States in late 1994. It had been engineered to stay fresh on the shelf for a longer time than the average tomato, holding its flavor well instead of becoming squishy and rotten. But opposition from farmers and consumers, along with problems growing the tomatoes on a large scale, eventually fed to the Flavr-Savr being withdrawn from the market.

Genetically modified foods are studied carefully in the contained, controlled surroundings of a greenhouse. This helps to reduce the risks of genes escaping into the environment.

still being researched while others are being test-grown in greenhouses or in field trials on small, carefully-controlled plots of land. The US Department of Agriculture (USDA) allowed testing on 4 GM crops in 1985, 1,194 in 2002, and over 12,000 in 2013.

Potential Risks of GM Foods

In theory, it is possible that new genes put into food plants and animals could damage the human body. Though there have been differing studies, there has not been *unequivocal* evidence that GM foods are harmful to humans. GM foods in the US also have to be approved by the Food and Drug Administration (FDA), but that does not mean that safety is always guaranteed.

Genes added to a food product, such as a farm crop, are intended to have certain effects—but they might also have other, unexpected effects. They could cause the plant to produce extra amounts of its natural chemicals. In normal amounts these cause no problems, but larger amounts might be poisonous. Or the new genes might make the plant produce unexpected substances which could be toxic or cause allergies.

Supporters of genetic engineering argue that millions of people have been eating GM foods for many years, and there are still no proven cases of direct harm being caused. Also, GM foods undergo extensive testing before distribution to the public. These trials are conducted in the laboratory, on animals, and on people who volunteer. Indeed, GM foods are tested far more than those made by traditional methods of selective breeding and have been found to be safe.

Identifying GM Foods

It can be relatively simple to identify "single" GM food products such as GM potatoes, oranges, or chickens. Many producers and supermarkets in the world already label them, so the consumer can choose whether or not to eat them. But foodstuffs such as maize and soy are bought, sold, mixed, and blended several times before being used as ingredients in sauces, gravies, pies, fillings, pizzas, and ready-cooked meals. It is not always easy, or even possible, to know if a processed or ready-cooked item contains GM foodstuffs. The US currently has no requirement to label these products, and while this may come in the future, doing so may increase the price of food.

Genes in the Wild

In most crops, the male parts of a flower release thousands of tiny pollen grains. They are blown by the wind or carried by creatures such as bees or birds to the female parts of a flower of the same species. A male cell in the pollen grain joins with a female cell in the flower to start the development of a new seed.

It is possible that male pollen grains from a GM plant could reach the female parts of a natural plant of the same species in another field. The new genes might get into the seeds of that plant and then be spread again by the pollen. In this way, the new gene could travel long distances, perhaps even across continents. The new gene might spread to the original wild version of the plant and change nature forever.

As we farm GM animals for food, it might turn out to be impossible to keep the "GMs" away from the "organics." A GM animal might interbreed with an organic one, allowing the new gene to gradually "escape" into the wild and spread into the natural population. The effects are unpredictable, so precautions are taken to prevent this from happening.

Scientists and farmers in the United States must go through several steps to test GM foods for safety in a controlled environment. At first, a new GM plant, such as GM wheat, is grown in a laboratory and then in larger numbers in a greenhouse. Plants are carefully studied to see if their growth is

Domesticated, rather than wild, forms of corn have spread to almost all areas of Mexico. Will new varieties of GM corn spread the same way, despite efforts to restrict them?

Those who operate organic farms are generally proud that their food crops are grown "the natural way," but they may worry that pollen from genetically modified (GMO) crops grown on nearby farms might be carried on the wind and affect their own crops.

healthy and whether they produce any unusual new substances. Their useful parts, such as the grains in wheat, are tested for ill-effects by feeding them to animals.

After the initial tests and studies have been completed for safety, the GM crop is grown in small batches in field trials. These field trials have to be carried out a certain distance from any non-GM fields of that crop. But studies show that some pollen grains can blow on the wind for at least 30 miles, and birds and bees can spread seeds and pollen even farther afield.

Possible Risks of Escaped Genes

The possibility that a gene might transfer from a properly-tested GM plant or animal into natural populations of plants and animals is exceedingly small. But the possible results, if this did occur, are far reaching. In a laboratory or greenhouse, there is an excellent chance of restricting the spread of a gene. But in the outside world, little can be done to halt it or get it back.

Suppose that a GM crop has a gene to resist a certain weed-killer spray. Out in the field, the crop suffers from a disease caused by a virus. Some of the viruses take up the gene from the crop and infect a weed nearby, passing the gene to the weed. The weed might then become a "super weed," resistant to the weed killer, and spread to cause huge damage. The exact same process of "carrier" viruses transferring genes from one type of living thing to another is used in genetic engineering itself.

Imagine another case involving animals: A "super pig" gene causes baby pigs to grow much bigger and faster. One day, one escapes and breeds with its natural cousin, the wild boar. The gene is passed, stage by stage, into the local wild boar population. This creates a new breed of "super boar" that wreaks havoc on the environment.

Recapturing Escaped Genes

Genetic-engineering supporters argue that the chances of genes escaping, jumping to other living things, and then actually working in them are so small as to be almost zero. But opponents compare the risk to the myth of the genie in the bottle: the genie promises to grant wishes, but the person who makes the wish does not think of all the possible consequences.

Opponents of genetic engineering say that once a new gene has escaped into nature, it can never be recaptured. Super weeds might smother the land, super bugs may spread plagues, and super animals could endanger lives. You cannot put the genie, or the gene, back in the bottle.

Anti-GMO Campaigns

In 1999 at several sites in the UK, anti-GM campaigners disrupted field trials of GM maize, chopping down and burning the plants. The field trials were legal and were following testing guidelines, but the protesters said the trials had been hushed up, and the dangers of the trials had not been resolved. In court, no protesters were found guilty of any offense.

Protests have continued to the present day. In 2012, hundreds of farmers in India gathered in peaceful protest of GM corn, not wanting their fields to be used for testing. They cited other countries where super weeds have spread as a result of genes from GM corn that are resistant to herbicides. In 2013, 400 protesters charged a field in the Philippines, where a field trial of the aforementioned golden rice was taking place. They uprooted and trampled the rice plants, saying the GM rice trial was a danger to human health and limiting to the natural diversity of crops.

Text-Dependent Questions

1. What are three ways GM crops can benefit people?
2. Provide one plant and one animal example of the risks of "escaped genes."

 # Research Project

Using the Internet or your school library, research the topic of GMO foods, and answer the following question: "Should companies in the US be required to label food products as GMO?"

Some contend that companies should have to label their products if there are GMOs in them. Even if foods are FDA approved, they are not completely natural and may have unknown health risks in the long-term. People should know what they are buying in general, and, particularly with food, they have a right to know if they are eating organic or genetically-modified foods.

Others argue that all foods approved by the FDA have been tested for safety, and GMOs are tested even more rigorously. There is no need to label every GM food product, which would unnecessarily raise the price of the food we buy. The supposed risks of GM foods are not validated by most scientists and may be a campaign by organic food companies to get people to buy more expensive organic products.

Write a two-page report, using data you have found in your research to support your conclusion, and present it to your class.

5

Cloning

Living things that have exactly the same genes as each other are called *clones*. Cloning involves manipulating or moving whole sets of genes. It does not necessarily involve genetic-engineering techniques such as adding or taking away individual genes. But there are some processes in cloning are used in genetic engineering and vice-versa.

Cloning happens in nature when identical twins are born. They come from the same egg cell, so they have exactly the same genes. Cloning has also been used for centuries by gardeners. They take part of a plant, such as a piece of stem, and grow it into a whole new plant that has the same exact genes as the parent—it is a clone.

Dolly the sheep was born in July 1996 in Edinburgh, Scotland. She was not the first clone of an animal, but she was

Identical twins have the same genes as each other. However, they develop their own individual personalities, likes and dislikes. They are not identical people.

the first mammal to be cloned from a specialized cell taken from an adult. Dolly showed that, in principle, any cell from any animal or plant, even an adult, could be used to make a clone.

The Cloning Process

Every microscopic cell in a living thing has a full set of the organism's genes. It is possible to take this full set out of its cell, as lengths of DNA, and put it into an egg cell that has had its own DNA removed. Inside this new "home," conditions are suited to all genes being "switched on," so they become the instructions for the whole living thing.

Until the mid-1990s, this could only be done with DNA removed from cells at a very early stage of development—*embryonic* cells from the growing mass that is formed when a fertilized egg splits to form new cells. When cloning cells at

 Words to Understand in This Chapter

biodiversity—the existence of many different kinds of plants and animals in an environment.

clone—a plant or animal that is grown from one cell of its parent and that has exactly the same genes as its parent.

embryo—a human or animal in the early stages of development before it is born, hatched, etc.

reproductive cloning—the cloning of organisms by planting a cell into the uterus of an adult female and thus creating a new organism.

therapeutic cloning—the creation of cloned human tissues for surgical transplant.

Dolly the sheep was the world's first animal to be cloned from an adult sheep cell, rather than from a fertilized egg. Dolly was cloned in 1996 and lived for almost seven years, before dying in February 2003 from a lung disease. This is fairly young by the usual standards, as sheep typically live to be 11 or 12 years old. However, scientists determined that her death was not a result of the cloning process. Since then, other animals have also been successfully cloned.

such an early stage of their development, it is not possible to predict the exact type of adults that will be produced. For example, when cloning the embryonic cells from a sheep, the hope might be that the cloned sheep will all have extra-quality wool, but this cannot be known for sure until the cloned sheep grow up into adults.

Cloning of Adult Cells

The answer to this problem is to clone body cells from an adult living thing rather than embryonic cells. But this raises a different problem: In a body cell from an adult, unlike a cell from an embryo, many of the genes are "switched off." Only a few are "on" because the cell is doing a specialized job in the adult body.

However, in the mid-1990s, methods were developed to "switch on" genes in a specialized adult cell. These methods include applying chemicals, heat, and electric currents to the cells as they grow in a flask or dish in the laboratory. Dolly the sheep was the first mammal to be produced this way.

Potential Benefits of Cloning

Clones of useful plants have been made for centuries. Today, many types of fruit, such as bananas and strawberries, are grown by cloning. Since the birth of Dolly the sheep, many clones of animals have also been made by scientists, ranging from frogs and mice to pigs and cows. Could a combination of genetic engineering and cloning help our future world? What are the costs and the risks?

There are many possible benefits of cloning. A champion egg-laying hen or milk-yielding cow might be cloned to give

These cows are, in effect, identical twins. But they were born to different mothers—they are clones. The aim of cloning is to produce exact genetic copies, so the animals themselves vary as little as possible.

thousands of offspring with the same genes. When these animals are produced by normal breeding methods, genetic variety occurs—some offspring are not quite so successful at the desired task, so production is lower. But with cloning, the animal's genes are copied exactly. Fruit can also be cloned to make replicas with their best traits.

Drawbacks to Cloning

Cloning does have drawbacks: To create Dolly, more than 270 attempts were made. They involved obtaining single cells from

The Human Genome Organization

In April 2003, scientists from the Human Genome Organization (HUGO) finished making the list of all the genetic material for a human being. This full set of genes is called the human genome. Bill Clinton, then president of the US, called it "the most wondrous map ever produced by mankind." Tony Blair, Prime Minister of the United Kingdom (UK), said it was "a breakthrough that opens the way for massive advancement." Though a major step was taken in genetics for humans, we still do not know exactly what each gene does or how it works.

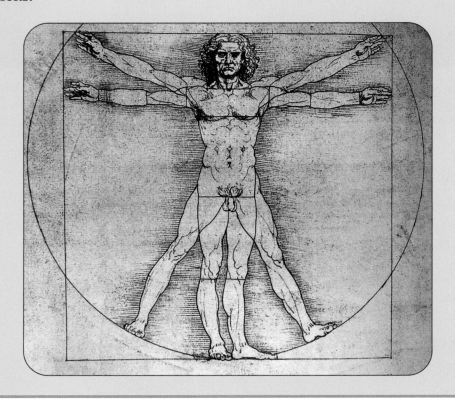

adult sheep, taking the genes out and activating them, and putting them into the wombs of female sheep. These cells behaved as egg cells and developed into newborn lambs. The losses represented many dead embryos and disrupted pregnancies.

In normal breeding, the variety in genes gives each individual a different resistance to disease. If a disease strikes a normally-bred flock or herd on a farm, some animals may die, but others might recover or even be unaffected. If the herd or flock is entirely made up of clones, one disease could wipe them all out since they have no genetic variety in disease resistance. The same applies to plants.

Natural breeding sometimes produces a new and useful feature—such as bigger grains in a wheat plant—by a chance change, or mutation, in the DNA. This is part of the idea of *biodiversity*—having a large, varied, and naturally changing collection of genes in a whole population of living things. If animals were made by cloning, new changes and combinations could not occur.

The Question of Human Cloning

The technology exists to make human clones and genetically engineer human cells. Cloned human embryos have in fact already been produced. Should this work continue, or are the consequences too dangerous?

Would human clones grow up to look and behave exactly the same as each other? If so, a top soldier might be cloned to produce a world-dominating army. In reality, clones may look the same, but they would not all behave the same: Identical twins are clones with the same genetic makeup. They look similar, but they have their own individual experiences and develop unique personalities. Even though they have the same genes, identical twins end up different to a degree.

Possible Benefits to Human Cloning

If a person develops a disease in one body part, cells might be taken out from another body part to help: In the laboratory, various genes in these cells could be switched on or off to make healthy new cells. These cloned cells could be grown into a new body part to replace the diseased one. Cells for this task could also have been taken from a person while they were still an embryo in the womb. These stem cells are easier to alter and manipulate than cells that are taken from an adult body.

Cloning of cells for the treatment of illness, rather than the growing of new human beings, is called *therapeutic cloning*. It could solve the problem of rejection in transplants. When a body part such as a kidney is transplanted from one person to another, the receiving body sometimes fights against this "foreign" part and tries to destroy it. This may not happen with therapeutic cloning.

Policies on Cloning

There is no worldwide agreement on whether the cloning of humans should be allowed. The laws and guidelines vary greatly from one country to another. In November 2001, the American company Advanced Cell Technology announced that it had produced the first fully-cloned human embryos. Such embryos would not be grown into human beings, but would provide cells for therapeutic cloning. In the same week, the British government moved to greatly limit all work on cloning human cells, including stem cells for medical use. Currently, there are no federal laws in the US regarding human cloning. There is a prohibition of spending federal money on human embryo research of any kind except in the case of embryonic stem cells created before August 9, 2001. Private funds, however, can be used to create embryos. Pro-life supporters view embryos as human beings, so they seek a ban on all cloning, including therapeutic. Others support a partial ban that would prohibit *reproductive cloning* to produce a human adult, but allows for therapeutic cloning.

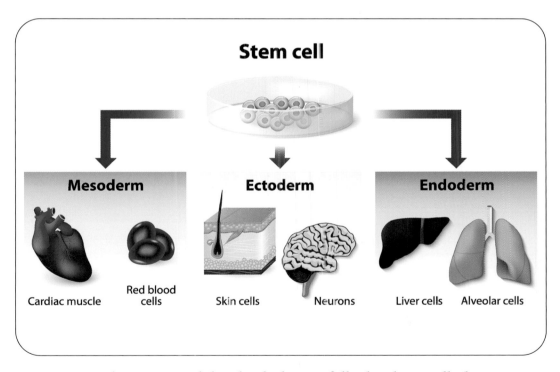

In 2014, researchers announced that they had successfully cloned stem cells that were genetically matched to adult patients. Stem cells are a type of cell that can be guided to produce any sort of body tissue or organ that needs to be replaced.

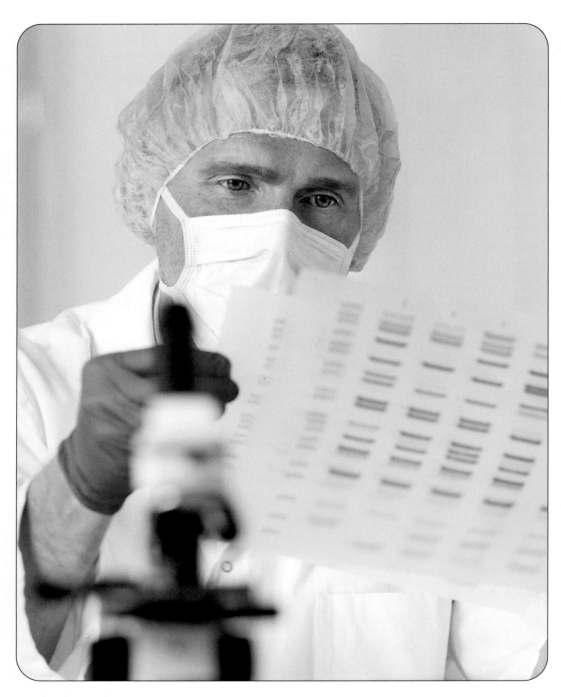

A scientist analyzes a DNA sequence.

More than 30 countries have banned reproductive cloning of humans. Some European countries, including France, Germany, and Switzerland, have banned cloning human embryos for reproductive or therapeutic purposes. England, Singapore, Sweden, China, and Israel allow cloning for research but not for reproduction.

 Text-Dependent Questions

1. Why is it more difficult to clone adult cells than embryonic cells? What methods are used to make it possible to clone adult cells?
2. What are three risks to cloning plants and animals?

 Research Project

Using the Internet or your school library, research the topic of reproductive human cloning, and answer the following question: "Should reproductive human cloning be allowed to create cloned living people?"

Some believe that if we have the technology to clone humans, we should be able to do it. If a couple is infertile, they can have a child that is biologically connected to them. Parents whose child dies could have that child "back" through cloning. Though human cloning is not developed or safe now, if it becomes safe, it is a right that people have to do what is within their means.

Others maintain that cloning humans should not be allowed because it would take away from the diversity of human life, which is a benefit to society. Cloning would lead to a culture where humans are treated as objects that can be manufactured and designed rather than created. It is also unsafe: most cloning attempts in animals lead to miscarriages, stillbirths, and risks to the carrying mother, and no humans should be put at risk in such ways.

Write a two-page report, using data you have found in your research to support your conclusion, and present it to your class.

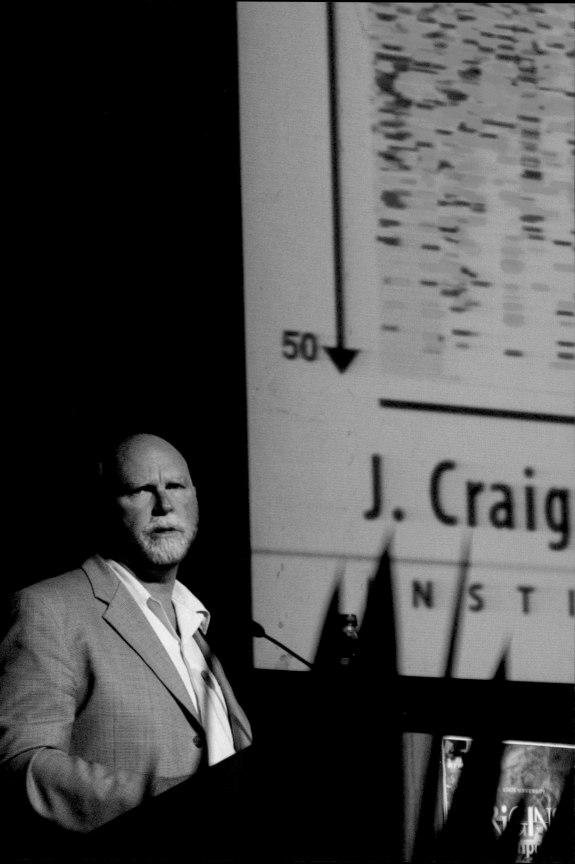

6

The Business of Genetic Engineering

R esearch into genetic engineering and other forms of genetics is a huge, worldwide business, and it is growing. The National Institutes of Health in the US estimated spending $7.9 billion on genetics research in 2015, and the numbers only expand in the scope of the entire world.

Funding Sources

Part of the money for genetic research comes from government organizations. This includes money set aside to find gene-based answers to major health problems for people, plants, and animals in the world. The richest nations, especially the US, spend the most.

Nearly all of the rest of the money comes from private sources. These vary from individual people to multinational

Dr. J Craig Venter, founder of Celera Genomics, speaks about sequencing the human genome at a seminar at Arizona State University. Celera Genomics of Rockville, Maryland, helped to speed up the work of the Human Genome Organization.

companies. In a few cases, people with extreme wealth donate money or set up a private project to find a genetic answer to a very specific problem. This might be a disease from which they or someone in their family suffers.

More than three-quarters of the money spent on genetics comes from private companies. As in any other business, a genetics company is set up to fill a need. If it does so, it makes a profit and continues. If not, the company goes bust. The biggest genetic engineering and biotechnology companies are based in the world's richest countries, mainly in the US, Europe, and Japan.

Reasons for Spending on Genetics

In many regions, genetic engineering is being used as part of the fight against terrible diseases such as malaria, typhoid, cholera, and AIDS. Genetic engineering could also help to make drinking water clean and pure by creating GMOs that are harmless to humans but kill the bugs that contaminate water. Genetic engineering could tackle the great levels of malnutri-

 Words to Understand in This Chapter

genome—one set of chromosomes with the genes they contain; the genetic material of an organism.

patent—the exclusive right granted by a government to an inventor to manufacture, use, or sell an invention or process for a certain number of years.

profit margin—the difference between the cost of buying or making something and the price at which it is sold.

For the Human Genome Project and beyond, thousands of samples of blood and other body parts are stored at -320°F (-196°C) in liquid nitrogen.

tion and death due to lack of food in parts of the world. It can make crops and farm animals yield more, create crops that grow in difficult conditions, and produce crops, such as golden rice, which contain extra vitamins. These benefits lead to cheaper and more nutritious foods.

In January 2001, Tewolde Berhan Egziabher, head of the Environmental Protection Authority of Ethiopia, convinced many developing countries to be cautious about a headlong rush into a GM world. He argued that permission to plant GM crops should not be immediately granted—but be postponed

Are anti-GM protesters saving us from genetic and environmental disaster, or ruining research that could help to feed the hungry and heal the sick?

until more studies on safety were conducted, and profits could be shared more fairly. This disappointed big businesses, which had hoped to make money from selling GM crops to poorer nations. Still, GMO companies forged ahead in other markets worldwide and are making enormous profits today. Monsanto, the world's largest seed company, made $14.9 billion in 2013 with a *profit margin* of 30 percent on their products sold.

Patenting Genes

People spend many years and large amounts of money inventing gadgets and machines, from cars to computers. Granting a *patent* to the inventors is seen as a fair way of rewarding them. The patent gives credit to the inventor as the originator of the idea and prevents others from using the invention unless they get permission and pay money to the person who owns the patent.

Patents also apply to genes. A genetic engineering company that "invents" a useful new combination of genes, such as a tomato that lasts longer on a store shelf, can be granted a patent. The patent for that combination of genes stops other people from simply copying it. If there were no patents, genetic engineering and biotechnology companies could not earn the money they need to survive.

The Human Genome Organization (HUGO) was set up in the late 1980s by various governments to begin the Human Genome Project, which aimed to map the entire human *genome*. At first, progress was slow, but in 1998, the commercial company Celera Genomics formed its own team to sequence the human genome. However, Celera controversially

Biotechnologists are trying to find an AIDS cure.

sought to keep some of the genome information under its own control for its own private use, as opposed to HUGO, which wanted to ensure that all information would be publicly available. A race ensued between HUGO and Celera, with the Human Genome Project completing its sequencing in 2003. Celera's project reached 92 percent completion in 2005 before the company moved on to other opportunities.

Claiming Gene Ownership

Of the 19,000 human genes, over 4,300 have been patented. In the US, there are some 47,000 patents on inventions involving genetic material. US companies hold the most genetic patents, followed by Europe and Japan. Many people in poorer countries see this as yet another example of the rich getting richer.

Patents are held not only on new combinations of genes, but on sets of genes that occur in a plant or animal in nature. Should a person or company be able to "own" such a natural, fundamental item as the instructions for life? Suppose a rare plant is discovered in the rain forest of a poor country. Scientists from a rich country could study the plant and find it has a useful gene for resisting disease. If they patent the gene and put it into a GM crop, they could make vast profits. Is this

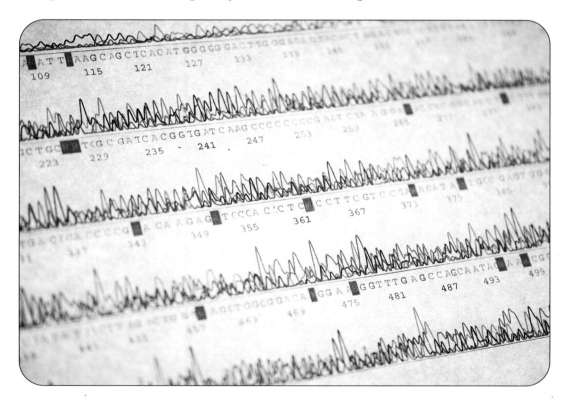

In 2013, the US Supreme Court ruled that the human genome could not be patented, but that synthetic DNA is patent eligible because it does not occur naturally.

fair? It could be argued that the genes belong to no individual or company but are part of nature, for everyone to share. But the scientists may claim they have done all the work, so do they deserve the reward?

In 2013, the US Supreme Court unanimously ruled that naturally occurring human genes could no longer be patented because they are simply discovered, not invented; the Supreme Court left room for patents on genes entirely created in the lab. In the case, *Association for Molecular Pathology vs. Myriad Genetics*, Myriad Genetics identified and isolated human BRCA genes in order to make a test to identify women at risk for breast cancer. Myriad argued the patents were justified after years of work put into identifying the genes, each containing a few thousand bases on chromosomes containing tens of millions of bases each. The Supreme Court ruling prevented Myriad from having a monopoly on BRCA genes and allowed for open research and commercial use of the genes by anyone. In contrast to the United States, an Australian federal court ruled in 2014 that discovered human genes can be awarded patents, showing the complexity of this new frontier.

Profiting from Genetics

Some people argue that genes are a product like any other. Companies chop down trees for lumber or make meat into hamburgers and sell them for profit. Some say genetic-engineering companies should be allowed to do the same with genes. A different argument is that genes are inside every one of us and in every living thing. They are, at the very basic level, life itself. No one should be allowed to own them, charge

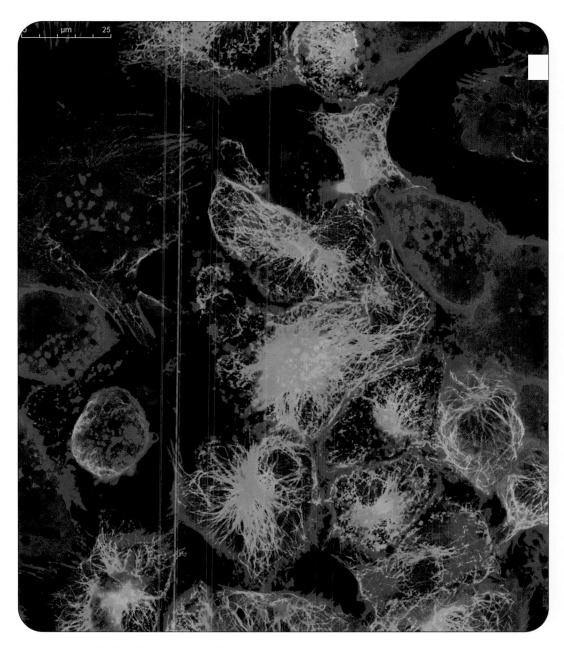

Cancerous cells, highlighted with fluorescent dye, as seen under a microscope. Inherited genetic mutations play a major role in about 5 to 10 percent of all cancers. Researchers have associated mutations in specific genes with more than 50 hereditary cancer syndromes, which are disorders that may predispose individuals to developing certain cancers.

money to use them, or make profits from them.

The pharmaceutical companies that develop and produce medicinal drugs do not simply want to help sick people. They are businesses that seek to make a profit, so that they can become wealthy and have money to develop more new drugs in the future. *Forbes* reported in 2013 that it takes, on average, $350 million to bring a new drug into general use, with 95 percent of experimental medicines failing to be effective and safe for humans. Even with such a cost, pharmaceutical companies make billions on a successful drug, with some costing $100,000 for one person to have a full course of a drug.

However, there is a complicated system of limits, licenses, and regulations that prevent companies from making "excessive" profits. These apply especially to medicinal drugs sold in poorer countries, which are often the places that most need but can least afford them. Perhaps similar controls should be applied to genetic engineering.

The Future of Genetic Engineering

Genetic engineering is a complex subject, and it is hard to tell how it will develop. It is also a very young science, barely 43 years old. Imagine if you could travel back in time to 1843, when the science of flowing electricity was only 43 years old. Some people at the time believed this new force was "the devil's work." Who could have predicted then how the world would one day depend on electricity?

In the future, genetic engineering might feed starving millions, ease the pain and suffering of millions more, and make the world a happier, healthier, safer place. Or, it might unleash nightmare diseases and superbugs, destroy vast areas of countryside, and make the rich even richer at the expense of the poor.

Evidence from other important advances in technology, such as cars, computers, and antibiotic drugs, suggests that the future may lie somewhere in between. It might depend not so much on the scientists and what they can do, but on society as a whole and what it wants science to achieve.

 # Text-Dependent Questions

1. What was controversial about Celera's pursuit of mapping the human genome?
2. Explain the 2013 Supreme Court decision on patenting human genes.

 # Research Project

Using the Internet or your school library, research the topic of genetic patents, and answer the following question: "Should there be patents on genes?"

Some think that there should not be gene patents because discovering something about a plant or animal does not means someone has the right to own part of it and make money off of it. Someone who first sees a star in the universe should not be able to own it since they did not create or invent it. Patenting genes makes an organism more of a product to be used than a life to be valued, and it prevents others from using the genes for the good of the public.

Others say that patents on genes should be allowed. It takes a great deal of work and money to do genetic research. The discoveries often come with benefits to masses of people and large amounts of profit. Those who take the time, energy, and money to do the research should have ownership of their work and have the freedom to make money from it. Otherwise, they may not pursue their research and not provide benefits to society.

Write a two-page report, using data you have found in your research to support your conclusion, and present it to your class.

Genetically Modified Foods Reference

GM Crops

For comparison, one hectare is an area 100 meters by 100 meters or one-hundredth of a square kilometer. It is 2.47 acres, approximately the size of two soccer fields. The total land area of the United States is approximately 937 million hectares, or 2,315,000,000 acres.

Global Area of GM Crops

Year	Area (Million Hectares)
1996	4.3
2000	109.2
2005	222.0
2010	365.0
2014	448.0

Source: International Service for the Acquisition of Agri-Biotech Applications (ISAAA), Global Status of Commercialized Biotech/GM Crops, 2014.

Global Area of GM Crops by Country in 2014

Country	Area (Million Hectares)
USA	73.1
Brazil	42.2
Argentina	24.3
India	11.6
Canada	11.6
China	3.9
Paraguay	3.9
Pakistan	2.9
South Africa	2.7
Uruguay	1.6
Bolivia	1.0

Source: ISAAA, Global Status of Commercialized
Biotech/GM Crops: 2014

Global Area of GM Crops in 2014 by Crop Type

GM Crop	Area (Million Hectares)	% of Total Crop
Soybean	90.7	82 %
Cotton	25.1	68 %
Maize (corn)	55.2	30 %
Canola	9.0	25 %
Total	*180.0*	*49 %*

Source: ISAAA, Global Status
of Commercialized Biotech/GM Crops: 2014

Genetically Modified Food Labeling Laws by Country

Official ban on GM food imports and cultivation: Benin, Serbia, Zambia

Mandatory labeling of nearly all GM foods and a labeling threshold of 0.9-1 percent GM content. Threshold refers to content per ingredient in each food item: Greenland, Iceland, Russia, Saudi Arabia, Turkey, Cyprus, Kazakhstan, Australia, New Zealand, and all European countries except Albania, Macedonia, Montenegro, Serbia

Mandatory labeling of many GM foods and a labeling threshold higher than 1 percent or undefined. This includes laws with a threshold of 1 percent for the entire food item: China, South Korea, Japan, Malaysia, Singapore, Indonesia, Sri Lanka, Ukraine, Kenya, Brazil

Mandatory labeling of some GM foods, but with numerous exceptions and no labeling threshold defined; or a vague mandatory GM food labeling law that lacks implementation and enforcement provisions: India, Thailand, Vietnam, Taiwan, Jordan, Tunisia, Ethiopia, Mali, Tunisia, Cameroon, Ecuador, Peru, Bolivia

No GM food labeling laws: All countries not listed above, including all of North America, most of Africa, and most of the Middle East.

Source: Center for Food Safety, 2016

Countries with Mandatory Labeling of Genetically-Engineered Foods

Australia	Iceland	Saudi Arabia
Austria	India	Senegal
Belarus	Indonesia	Slovakia
Belgium	Ireland	Slovenia
Bolivia	Italy	South Africa
Bosnia and	Japan	South Korea
Herzegovina	Jordan	Spain
Brazil	Kazakhstan	Sri Lanka
Bulgaria	Kenya	Sweden
Cameroon	Latvia	Switzerland
China	Lithuania	Taiwan
Croatia	Luxembourg	Thailand
Cyprus	Malaysia	Tunisia
Czech Republic	Mali	Turkey
Denmark	Malta	Ukraine
Ecuador	Mauritius	United Kingdom
El Salvador	Netherlands	Vietnam
Estonia	New Zealand	
Ethiopia	Norway	
Finland	Peru	
France	Poland	
Germany	Portugal	
Greece	Romania	
Hungary	Russia	

Source: Center for Food Safety, 2016

Human Genome Timeline

1988   HUGO (Human Genome Organization) is founded by scientists from around the world.

1990   The Human Genome Project begins.

1992   The first general map shows the way in which many genes are linked.

1995   First detailed gene maps are made for chromosomes, numbers 16 and 19.

1996   Mapping is completed for the whole set of genes activated in a human cell—in this case, a type of white blood cell.

1997   Very detailed maps are made for chromosomes 7 and X (female sex chromosome).

1998   First genome base sequence map is completed for a multi-celled living thing, a worm (Caenorhabditis elegans).

1999   First complete map is completed for one human chromosome, number 22.

2000 Completion of first "working draft" of human genome DNA sequence.

2001 February: initial working draft sequence for DNA is published.

2003 Human Genome Project completion announced.

Genetics, Biotechnology, and Cloning Timeline

1866   Austrian Gregor Mendel's tests on peas lay foundations for science of genetics.

1900   Drosophila (fruit flies) used in early studies of genes.

1938   Hans Spemann suggests cloning by taking nucleus of one cell and inserting it into an egg cell with nucleus removed.

1940   DNA shown to be the substance that carries genes.

1953   Watson and Crick describe the double-helix structure of DNA.

1966   The genetic code is cracked, showing which codes of bases in DNA produce which products.

1967   The substance DNA ligase is isolated, which "glues" pieces of DNA together.

1970   The first artificial gene is made by gluing pieces of DNA. Restriction enzymes are used to cut and splice pieces of DNA.

1973   Improved DNA techniques produce the first recombinant DNA (gene-spliced) organism, a new variety of E.

coli bacteria.

1976 First research begins on genetic engineering in human-inherited disease. Methods of DNA sequencing discovered.

1978 Human insulin is first produced by genetic engineering. Louise Brown becomes the first "test-tube baby" (conceived outside the mother's body).

1979 Human growth hormone is made by artificial means.

1981 The first transgenic animals—with genes from other animals—are mice.

1983 Polymerase chain reaction (PCR) technique is used to make unlimited copies of DNA. Genetic "markers" are discovered for inherited diseases.

1984 DNA fingerprinting technique developed. The first genetically-engineered vaccine is made. An entire genome is sequenced for the AIDS virus HIV. Sheep become the first mammals cloned from embryonic cells.

1985 Genetically-engineered plants are tested for resistance to insects, viruses, and bacteria.

1986 The first field tests for genetically-engineered plants are conducted on tobacco.

1988 The first American patent for a genetically-altered animal is given.

1990 Artificially-produced chymosin for cheese making is the first product of genetic engineering approved for the human food industry in the US. Gene-therapy treatment is performed successfully on a four-year-old girl. A genetically altered cow produces human milk proteins for human babies.

1993 The first human cells, taken from embryos, are cloned.

1994 The Flavr-Savr tomato is the first genetically-engineered whole food approved for sale in the US. The first breast cancer gene is discovered. Calves are cloned from cells of early embryos.

1996 The gene associated with Parkinson's disease is discovered. Dolly the sheep is the first mammal cloned from the specialized cell of an adult sheep.

1997 The first herbicide- and insect-resistant crops introduced on a large scale.

1998 Experiments with cell-repair genes show human life may be extended 40%.

2000 A cloned cow shows that cloning can rejuvenate cells. Biotechnology study focuses on human aging problems.

2001 President George W. Bush supports research on stem cells. The UK moves to greatly restrict work on human cloning. The American company ACT announces the growing of cloned human embryos to six-cell stage, solely for therapeutic uses (medical treatments).

2002 Genetically-altered and cloned pigs suggest this research could provide "spare-part" organs for human transplants. Dolly the sheep has arthritis, which would normally occur in a much older sheep (is she as old as herself and her clone added together?).

2003 Human Genome Project completes sequencing of the entire human genome.

2005 Chimpanzee genome sequenced, allowing comparison between human and chimpanzee genomes.

2009 First complete cancer genomes sequenced, revealing differences between normal and cancerous tissue.

2012 Denisovan (ancient human species) genome sequenced from a bone and two teeth found in Siberia. The sequenced genome was from a Denisovan girl who lived 80,000 years ago.

Organizations
to Contact

Center for Food Safety

660 Pennsylvania Avenue, SE, #302

Washington, DC 20003

http://www.centerforfoodsafety.org/

**International Service for the Acquisition
of Agri-Biotech Applications**

105 Leland Lab

Cornell University, Ithaca

New York 14853

http://www.isaaa.org/default.asp

Centre for Research on Globalization (CRG)

PO Box 55019

11 Notre-Dame Ouest

Montreal, Qc, H2Y 4A7

http://www.globalresearch.ca/theme/science-and-medicine

The American Society of Gene Therapy

555 East Wells Street, Suite 1100
Milwaukee, WI 53202
www.asgt.org

The Council for Responsible Genetics

5 Upland Road, Suite 3
Cambridge, MA 02140
www.gene-watch.org

National Institutes of Health

9000 Rockville Pike
Bethesda, Maryland 20892
http://www.nih.gov/

Wellcome Trust Sanger Institute

Hinxton, Cambridge
CB10 1SA, UK
http://www.sanger.ac.uk/

Series Glossary

apartheid—literally meaning "apartness," the political policies of the South African government from 1948 until the early 1990s designed to keep peoples segregated based on their color.

BCE and CE—alternatives to the traditional Western designation of calendar eras, which used the birth of Jesus as a dividing line. BCE stands for "Before the Common Era," and is equivalent to BC ("Before Christ"). Dates labeled CE, or "Common Era," are equivalent to *Anno Domini* (AD, or "the Year of Our Lord").

colony—a country or region ruled by another country.

democracy—a country in which the people can vote to choose those who govern them.

detention center—a place where people claiming asylum and refugee status are held while their case is investigated.

ethnic cleansing—an attempt to rid a country or region of a particular ethnic group. The term was first used to describe the attempt by Serb nationalists to rid Bosnia of Muslims.

house arrest—to be detained in your own home, rather than in prison, under the constant watch of police or other government forces, such as the army.

reformist—a person who wants to improve a country or an institution, such as the police force, by ridding it of abuses or faults.

republic—a country without a king or queen, such as the US.

United Nations—an international organization set up after the end of World War II to promote peace and co-operation throughout the world. Its predecessor was the League of Nations

UN Security Council—the permanent committee of the United Nations that oversees its peacekeeping operations around the world.

World Bank—an international financial organization, connected to the United Nations. It is the largest source of financial aid to developing countries.

World War I—A war fought in Europe from 1914 to 1918, in which an alliance of nations that included Great Britain, France, Russia, Italy, and the United States defeated the alliance of Germany, Austria-Hungary, the Ottoman Empire, and Bulgaria.

World War II—A war fought in Europe, Africa, and Asia from 1939 to 1945, in which the Allied Powers (the United States, Great Britain, France, the Soviet Union, and China) worked together to defeat the Axis Powers (Germany, Italy, and Japan).

Further Reading

Carey, Nessa. *The Epigenetics Revolution: How Modern Biology Is Rewriting Our Understanding of Genetics, Disease, and Inheritance*. New York: Columbia University Press, 2013.

Cooper, James. *Food Myths Debunked: Why Our Food Is Safe*. Wilton, CT: Fairfield Easton Press, 2014.

Knoepfler, Paul. *Stem Cells: An Insider's Guide*. Singapore: World Scientific Publishing Company, 2013.

Lott, Joey. *Natural Deception: A Sobering Look at the Truth behind the Organic Food Industry*. Digital: Archangel Ink, 2015.

Mphil, Claire Robinson, Michael Antoniou, and John Fagan. *GMO Myths and Truths: A Citizen's Guide to the Evidence on the Safety and Efficacy of Genetically Modified Crops and Foods*. White River Junction, VT: Chelsea Green Publishing, 2015.

Slack, Jonathan. *Stem Cells: A Very Short Introduction*. New York: Oxford University Press, 2012.

Internet Resources

www.isaaa.org/default.asp

Articles, data, and facts that promote GM foods from the International Service for the Acquisition of Agri-Biotech Applications.

www.gmo-compass.org/eng/home

GMO Compass provides a wide variety of GMO information on topics such as grocery shopping, human health, and environmental safety.

www.gmwatch.org

GM Watch gives the latest news and comment on GM foods and crops with articles and videos in opposition to the GM industry.

www.geneticsandsociety.org/index.php

Center for Genetics and Society's website on stem cell research, cloning, and genetic engineering on animals. Includes policies on genetics at the federal and state levels in the US, as well as regulations in other countries.

www.genome.gov/10001772

National Human Genome Research Institute's information on the human genome, including a timeline, overview of the Human Genome Project, and implications for the future.

www.genengnews.com

This portal site provides links to articles and news reports about genetic engineering and biotechnology.

https://ghr.nlm.nih.gov

The National Institutes of Health manages this Genetics Home Reference page, which provides consumer-friendly information about the effects of genetic variations on human health.

www.hugo-international.org

Official website of the Human Genome Organisation, the international organisation of scientists involved in research into human genetics.

Index

Numbers in **_bold italics_** refer to captions.

About the Author

Martin Thompson has written numerous articles and essays on biology and genetics. He attended Iowa State University, and currently works as a teacher and freelance editor in Des Moines. This is his first book.